NEW DAD,

SAME BAD JOKES

NEW DAD, SAME BAD JOKES

A DAD JOKE A DAY FOR THAT FIRST SLEEPLESS YEAR

★

SLADE WENTWORTH

ZEITGEIST | NEW YORK

Published in the United States by Zeitgeist,
an imprint of Zeitgeist™, a division of
Penguin Random House LLC, New York.

penguinrandomhouse.com

Zeitgeist™ is a trademark of
Penguin Random House LLC

ISBN: 9780593436011
Ebook ISBN: 9780593435816

Author photograph © by Daxson Wentworth

Cover art © by Malchev/Shutterstock.com
Interior art © Primsky/Shutterstock.com
and K1r1/Shutterstock.com

Book design by Aimee Fleck
Edited by Erin Nelson

Printed in the United States of America

1 3 5 7 9 10 8 6 4 2

First Edition

FOR CADE AND DAXSON.
MOM AND I ARE PROUD OF YOU.
NOW GO BRUSH YOUR TEETH.

CONGRATULATIONS, DAD!

Welcome to a life that is no longer your own. As a father of two, I remember the joys and strains of those early months, from the beauty of a babbling smile to the trauma of a bathtub turd. Surviving the sleepless nights and thriving as a dad-hero requires learning new stress-reducing tricks and techniques. That's why this book is full of the most tried-and-true fatherly resources ever invented: dad jokes.

In these pages, you'll find a mix of baby jokes and classic eye rollers—enough for every day of that first wild and wonderful year. Use them as a marker for each time you make it to the next day, or simply surprise your loved ones with a few knee-slapping LOLs when the moment strikes.

The most important part of this book? You do you. Go in order, or flip through these pages and find what suits your mood. Along the way, you'll see humorous hacks and writing prompts to make the most of your new-dad adventures.

Your baby may be new, but these jokes are *full-groan*. Have fun, and take a load off, Dad. You're about to earn it.

DAY 1

Q: What do you call a newborn baby?

A: Anything you want.

• • • • • • • • • • • •

DAY 2

I heard my cousin was in the hospital and couldn't walk or speak. I was so worried, I rushed to visit. Apparently, all newborns are like that.

• • • • • • • • • • • •

DAY 3

Q: When does a joke become a dad joke?

A: When it becomes apparent.

• • • • • • • • • • • •

DAY 4

New dads seem to get sick only on weekdays. They must have a weekend immune system.

DAY 5

A woman in labor suddenly shouted, "Shouldn't! Wouldn't! Didn't! Can't!" The concerned father-to-be asked, "Doctor, what's going on?" "Don't worry," replied the doctor. "Those are just contractions."

• • • • • • • • • • • •

DAY 6

Q: What does the sourdough dad do at night?

A: Tells breadtime stories.

• • • • • • • • • • • •

DAY 7

Q: Where does the dad pig leave his car?

A: The porking lot.

DAY 8

My newborn son made such a fuss
when the doctor cut his umbilical cord.
He had really grown attached to it.

• • • • • • • • • • • •

DAY 9

Q: What does a baby computer call its father?

A: Data.

• • • • • • • • • • • •

DAY 10

Q: When is a door not a door?

A: When it's ajar.

• • • • • • • • • • • •

DAY 11

Of all the inventions of the past 100 years,
the dry-erase board is the most remarkable.

DAY 12

Q: Why did the kids take scissors to their joke book?

A: Dad told them to cut the comedy.

• • • • • • • • • • • •

DAY 13

Q: How did the baby know she was ready to be born?

A: She was running out of womb.

DAD HACK: Learn how to swaddle your baby, which gives most newborns a sense of security and comfort. You can find excellent how-to videos on the internet. In a pinch, videos on how to fold a burrito also work well.

DAY 14

Q: What did the mama snake say to her sick baby?

A: "Poor thing, let's viper nose!"

• • • • • • • • • • • •

DAY 15

Q: What's the difference between a baby and a baked potato?

A: About 140 calories.

• • • • • • • • • • • •

DAY 16

Q: What do you call a line of dads waiting to get haircuts?

A: A barberqueue.

DAY 17

Q: Why did the mom demand a paycheck from the hospital?

A: To compensate her for her labor.

• • • • • • • • • • • •

DAY 18

We were shocked by the bill we received from the hospital. We felt nickeled-and-dimed at every turn. They even charged us extra for heat. It was so uncool.

• • • • • • • • • • • •

DAY 19

Q: What's the dad pig's favorite position in baseball?

A: Shortslop.

DAY 20

Q: Why did the vampire baby stop eating baby food?

A: He wanted something to sink his teeth into.

• • • • • • • • • • • •

DAY 21

When the new dad read "16 to 28 pounds" on the side of the diaper box, he said, "Wow, these hold incredibly huge bowel movements."

• • • • • • • • • • • •

DAY 22

Q: Why do we dress babies in onesies?

A: They can't dress themselves, now, can they?

DAY 23

I sat next to a baby on a 10-hour flight. I didn't think it was possible for someone to cry for 10 hours straight. Even the baby was impressed I pulled it off.

• • • • • • • • • • • •

DAY 24

Q: How do you know when you've slept like a baby?

A: When you've woken up every two hours and cried.

• • • • • • • • • • • •

DAY 25

Q: What do a tick and the Eiffel Tower have in common?

A: They're both Paris sites.

DAY 26

If a baby refuses to nap, is he guilty of resisting a rest?

DAY 27

Q: Why does a mother carry her baby?

A: The baby can't carry the mother, now, can it?

DAY 28

I used to dislike facial hair, but then it started to grow on me.

DAD HACK: To catch up on sleep, take the advice that's often given to new moms: sleep when the baby sleeps. You can also prepare dinner when the baby prepares dinner and mow the lawn when the baby mows the lawn.

DAY 29

Dear Math,
Please grow up and solve
your own problems.

• • • • • • • • • • • •

DAY 30

Today I decided to go visit my childhood home. I asked the residents if I could come inside because I was feeling nostalgic, but they refused and slammed the door in my face. My parents are the worst.

• • • • • • • • • • • •

DAY 31

Q: Where do boats go when they get sick?

A: The boat doc, of course.

DAY 32

Q: What did one wall say to the other?

A: I'll meet you at the corner.

• • • • • • • • • • • •

DAY 33

I have a joke about construction,
but I'm still working on it.

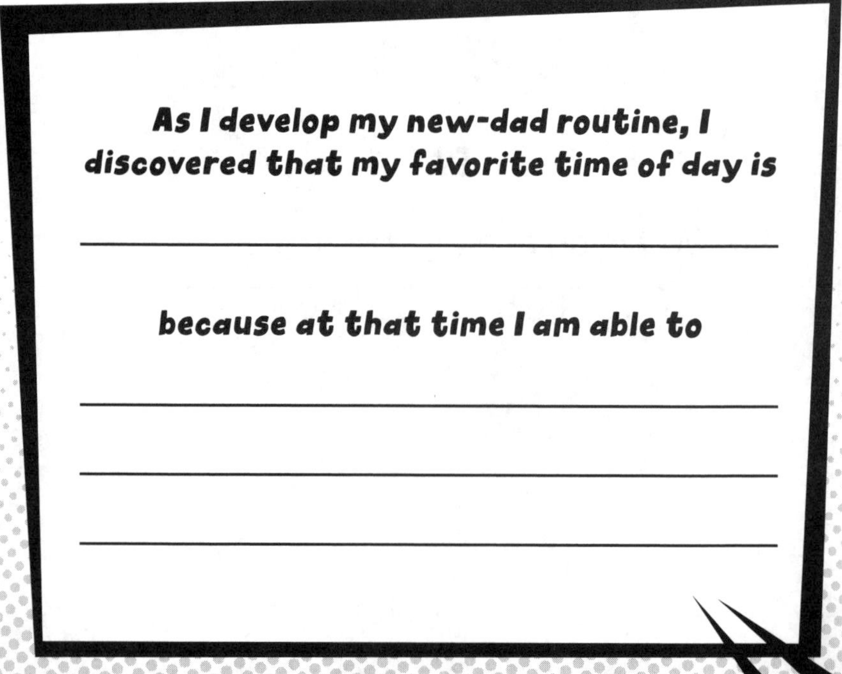

DAY 34

Q: Have you heard about the pregnant bedbug?

A: She's going to have her baby in the spring.

• • • • • • • • • • • •

DAY 35

Q: Why is that baby still in diapers?

A: I'll give you two reasons: number one and number two.

• • • • • • • • • • • •

DAY 36

We all know about Murphy's Law: anything that can go wrong will go wrong. But have you ever heard of Cole's Law? It's thinly sliced cabbage.

DAY 37

Q: Have you considered reading a book of prime numbers to the baby?

A: You'll have their undivided attention.

DAY 38

A friend came to me for advice and asked whether she should have a baby after 40. I said that I didn't think so; 40 babies are probably enough.

DAY 39

Q: Have you heard my joke about nepotism?

A: Sorry, I only tell it to my kids.

DAY 40

A turtle is crossing the road when he's mugged by two snails. When the police ask him what happened, the shaken turtle replies, "I don't know. It all happened so fast."

DAY 41

It's easy to convince moms not to eat Tide Pods, but it's harder to deter gents.

DAY 42

A skeleton walks into a bar and says, "Bartender, I'll have one beer and a mop."

DAD HACK: If your baby hates tummy time, make it more enjoyable by plopping them on your chest. Enjoy your first face-to-face conversations with your child.

DAY 43

Q: Do you know why baby girls are more likely to be born on holidays?

A: There's no mail delivery on holidays.

• • • • • • • • • • • •

DAY 44

The nurse told the parents of a newborn, "You have a cute baby." The smiling husband said, "I bet you say that to all the new parents." "No," she replied. "Just to parents of actually cute babies." The husband asked, "So, what do you say to the others?" The nurse replied, "The baby looks just like you."

• • • • • • • • • • • •

DAY 45

I was fed up with my wife's accusation that I have a poor sense of direction. So, I packed up my stuff and right.

DAY 46

I got carded at the liquor store, and my Blockbuster card accidentally fell out of my wallet. The cashier said, "Never mind."

• • • • • • • • • • • •

DAY 47

Q: Did you hear the rumor about the butter?

A: Well, I'm not going to spread it.

• • • • • • • • • • • •

DAY 48

I don't trust those trees. They seem shady.

• • • • • • • • • • • •

DAY 49

I don't trust those stairs. They're up to something.

DAY 50

My partner is so unfair. I remembered the car seat, the stroller, and the diaper bag. All she can talk about is how I forgot the baby.

• • • • • • • • • • • •

DAY 51

My wife and I have decided not to have kids. The kids aren't taking it well.

• • • • • • • • • • • •

DAY 52

MOM: Why is there a strange baby in the crib?

DAD: You told me to change the baby.

• • • • • • • • • • • •

DAY 53

Q: What do you call a group of baby soldiers?

A: An infantry.

DAY 54

JACK: Your mom is having a new baby?

JILL: Yes.

JACK: What's wrong with the old one?

• • • • • • • • • • • • •

DAY 55

Q: What do you do when you see a baby spinning in circles?

A: Stop laughing, and untie them from the ceiling fan.

DAD HACK: Record every time your baby sleeps and eats. At the end of each month, you'll have created tables you can make graphs of to show their progress. And at the end of the first year, a summary PowerPoint presentation isn't out of the question.

DAY 56

Do I enjoy making courthouse puns? Guilty.

DAY 57

I'm reading an antigravity book.
It's impossible to put down!

DAY 58

Q: What is the difference between a man and childbirth?

A: One can be terribly painful and is sometimes almost unbearable, while the other is just having a baby.

• • • • • • • • • • • •

DAY 59

Q: Why couldn't the bicycle stand up by itself?

A: It was two tired.

• • • • • • • • • • • •

DAY 60

DAUGHTER: Dad, can you put on my shoes?

DAD: No, I don't think they'll fit me.

• • • • • • • • • • • •

DAY 61

My baby just ate a bunch of Scrabble tiles. The next diaper change could spell disaster.

DAY 62

Q: Who's bigger: Mrs. Bigger, Mr. Bigger, or their baby?

A: Their baby—he's a little Bigger.

• • • • • • • • • • • •

DAY 63

A couple is having a baby soon. After learning they're having a boy, the husband says, "Let's name him Pete!" But the wife says, "Honey, we're having twins." The husband replies, "Well, we can call the second one Repeat."

• • • • • • • • • • • •

DAY 64

I was fired from my job at the calendar printer just because I took a couple of days off.

DAY 65

SON: Dad, can you put the dog out?

DAD: The dog's on fire?!

• • • • • • • • • • • •

DAY 66

I found a wooden shoe in my toilet today. It was totally clogged.

• • • • • • • • • • • •

DAY 67

Changing diapers is the hardest part about having kids. You can't half-ass it.

• • • • • • • • • • • •

DAY 68

I just watched a documentary series about beavers. It was the best dam show I've seen all year.

DAY 69

Q: Do I have to have a baby shower?

A: Not if you change their diaper quickly.

• • • • • • • • • • • •

DAY 70

I saw a baby owl caught in the rain. It was a moist owlet.

• • • • • • • • • • • •

DAY 71

Q: How does a salad say grace?

A: "Lettuce pray."

DAD HACK: If your baby has a cold, you can reduce their congestion by elevating their head while they sleep. This is best done by placing books underneath the head-side legs of their crib. Bonus: Using dictionaries will develop their vocabulary.

DAY 72

Last night I dreamed I was a muffler. I woke up exhausted.

• • • • • • • • • • • •

DAY 73

Q: Did you hear about the baby who got kicked out of the theater?

A: She yelled, "Pacifire!"

• • • • • • • • • • • •

DAY 74

A guy walks into a bar. Disqualified from the limbo contest.

• • • • • • • • • • • •

DAY 75

Q: Did you hear about the snowman who threw a tantrum?

A: It was a real meltdown.

DAY 76

Q: How much room is needed for fungi to grow?

A: As mushroom as possible.

. . . .

DAY 77

I have a joke about chemistry, but I don't think it will get a reaction.

. . . .

DAY 78

Q: Did you hear about the $0.45 concert?

A: It's 50 Cent featuring Nickelback.

. . . .

DAY 79

Q: Did you hear about the stolen cheddar?

A: A classic case of nacho cheese.

DAY 80

Swimming with sharks is expensive. Cost me an arm and a leg.

• • • • • • • • • • • •

DAY 81

Q: How did it work out for the lady who had a sea section?

A: She gave birth to a bouncing baby buoy.

• • • • • • • • • • • •

DAY 82

Shout-out to my fingers. I can count on all of them.

• • • • • • • • • • • •

DAY 83

Q: Did you hear about the baby who made a tissue dance?

A: He put a little boogie in it.

DAY 84

People say you pick your nose, but
I feel like I was born with mine.

DAY 85

Q: If you have 13 apples in one hand and 10 oranges in the other, what do you have?

A: Big hands.

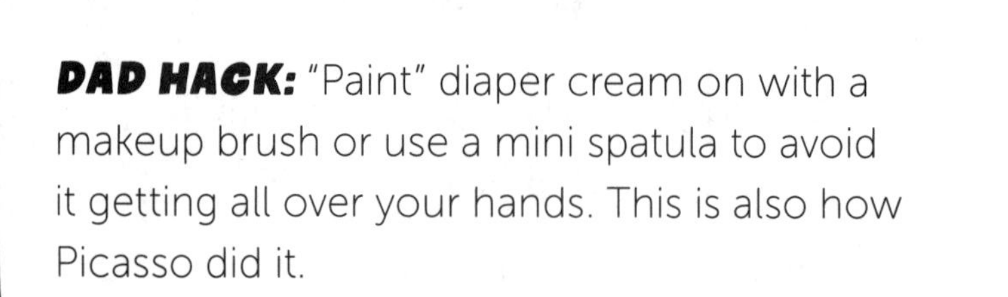

DAD HACK: "Paint" diaper cream on with a makeup brush or use a mini spatula to avoid it getting all over your hands. This is also how Picasso did it.

DAY 86

Q: What did the buffalo say to his son when he dropped him off at school?

A: "Bison."

• • • • • • • • • • • •

DAY 87

A kid decided to burn his house down. His dad watched, tears in his eyes. He put his arm around his wife and said, "That's arson."

• • • • • • • • • • • •

DAY 88

I didn't want to believe that my dad was stealing from his job as a road worker. But when I got home, all the signs were there.

DAY 89

Q: Did you hear about the bees with sticky hair?

A: Classic case of honeycomb.

• • • • • • • • • • • •

DAY 90

My partner dared me to name our daughter something ridiculous, so I'm calling her Bluff.

Our favorite nicknames for the baby are

____

and

____

I promise never to call them

____

DAY 91

Q: How do light bulbs say good night?

A: "I love you watts and watts."

• • • • • • • • • • • •

DAY 92

I was once addicted to the Hokey Pokey, but I was able to turn myself around.

• • • • • • • • • • • •

DAY 93

Q: What country's capital is growing the fastest?

A: Ireland. Every day it's Dublin.

• • • • • • • • • • • •

DAY 94

Q: What's the difference between a baby and a salad?

A: Most people don't get upset when you toss a salad.

DAY 95

I used to play the piano by ear.
Now I use my hands.

• • • • • • • • • • • • • •

DAY 96

Bad puns are how eye roll.

• • • • • • • • • • • • • •

DAY 97

Q: What's the leading cause of dry skin?

A: Towels.

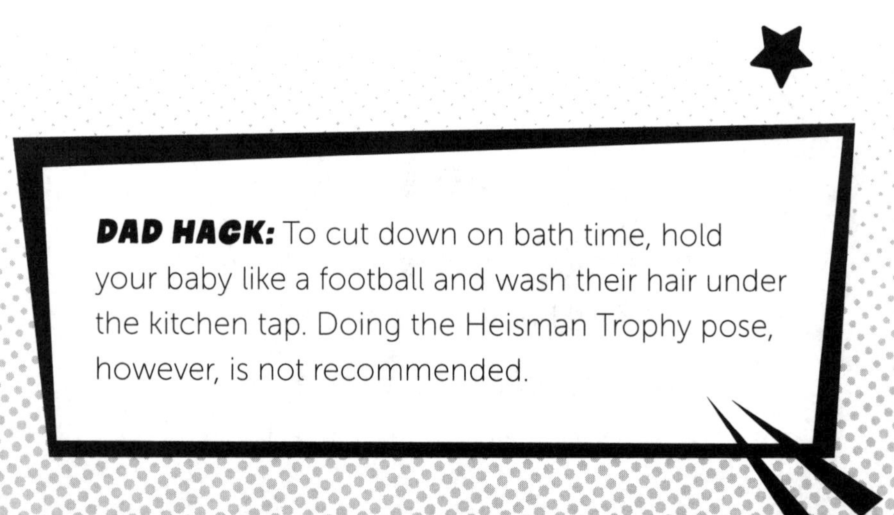

DAD HACK: To cut down on bath time, hold your baby like a football and wash their hair under the kitchen tap. Doing the Heisman Trophy pose, however, is not recommended.

DAY 98

I got a hen to count her own eggs. She's a real mathemachicken!

• • • • • • • • • • • •

DAY 99

Q: Why do dogs run in circles?

A: It's easier than running in triangles.

• • • • • • • • • • • •

DAY 100

A friend asked, "Why don't you stop writing just a bunch of jokes and start writing an actual book?" I replied, "That's a novel idea."

• • • • • • • • • • • •

DAY 101

I'm making a collection of candy canes for my newborn. They are all in mint condition.

DAY 102

Lately, people have been making apocalypse jokes like there's no tomorrow.

• • • • • • • • • • • •

DAY 103

Q: Did you hear about the scarecrow award?

A: Outstanding in its field.

• • • • • • • • • • • •

DAY 104

MOM: Do you think our kid is spoiled?

DAD: No, I think they all smell like that.

• • • • • • • • • • • •

DAY 105

Long fairy tales tend to dragon.

DAY 106

Q: What kind of dogs do babies love most?

A: Toy breeds.

• • • • • • • • • • • •

DAY 107

Little Sam was in the bath, and his mom was washing his hair. She said to him, "Wow, your hair is growing so fast! You need a haircut again." Sam replied, "Maybe you should stop watering it so much."

• • • • • • • • • • • •

DAY 108

Q: Why did the can crusher quit his job?

A: It was soda pressing.

DAY 109

Q: What time did the dad go to the dentist?

A: Tooth hurt-y.

• • • • • • • • • • • • • •

DAY 110

Poop jokes aren't my favorite jokes,
but they're a solid number two.

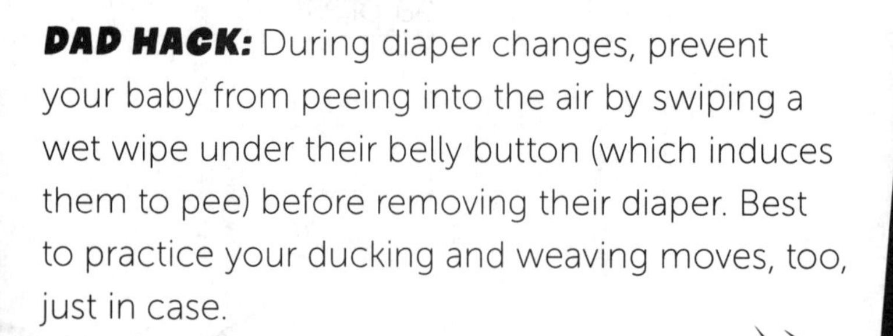

DAD HACK: During diaper changes, prevent your baby from peeing into the air by swiping a wet wipe under their belly button (which induces them to pee) before removing their diaper. Best to practice your ducking and weaving moves, too, just in case.

DAY 111

Q: What do you call an elephant that doesn't matter?

A: An irrelephant.

• • • • • • • • • • • •

DAY 112

Q: What is faster: hot or cold?

A: Hot. You can always catch a cold.

• • • • • • • • • • • •

DAY 113

Q: Why did the man bring his pregnant partner a small lizard?

A: She told him to pick up a baby monitor.

DAY 114

A robber walked into a bank and shouted, "Give me all the money in the safe, or you're geography!" The bank tellers looked at each other, confused. "Don't you mean 'history'?" one of them asked. "Don't change the subject!" the robber yelled back.

DAY 115

Q: How do you row a canoe filled with puppies?

A: You use a doggy paddle.

• • • • • • • • • • • •

DAY 116

I used to be a personal trainer. Then I put in my too-weak notice.

• • • • • • • • • • • •

DAY 117

DAUGHTER: Dad, what did you call your security blanket when you were little?

DAD: I'm drawing a blankie.

• • • • • • • • • • • •

DAY 118

Q: Did you hear about the guy who ironed his four-leaf clover?

A: Really pressed his luck.

DAY 119

I ordered a chicken and an egg online. I'll let you know.

• • • • • • • • • • • •

DAY 120

I tried to steal candy from a newborn baby, but he slapped my hand away. Turns out he wasn't born yesterday.

• • • • • • • • • • • •

DAY 121

Q: Why is Saturday the strongest day?

A: That's when the weak ends.

• • • • • • • • • • • •

DAY 122

Q: What do you call a polite bridge builder?

A: A civil engineer.

DAY 123

My least favorite color is purple. I like it less than red and blue combined.

• • • • • • • • • • • •

DAY 124

Q: What do you call a cow that's had a baby?

A: De-calf-inated.

DAD HACK: To burp your baby, hold them upright with their head on your shoulder. Support their head while gently patting their back with your other hand. If the burp is loud, celebrating with a gentle fist pump is optional but highly recommended.

DAY 125

Q: Why is a computer so smart?

A: It listens to its motherboard.

• • • • • • • • • • • •

DAY 126

Going to the barbeque? Don't forget the pickle. It's kind of a big dill.

• • • • • • • • • • • •

DAY 127

I was shopping in a bookstore and couldn't find what I was looking for. The shopkeeper said, "Can I help you, sir?" "Sure," I responded. "Can you help me find a play by Shakespeare?" "Which one?" the shopkeeper asked. "Um," I answered, surprised he didn't know. "William."

DAY 128

Q: What did the dad tomato say to the baby tomato?

A: "Ketchup!"

• • • • • • • • • • • •

DAY 129

It takes real guts to be an organ donor.

• • • • • • • • • • • •

DAY 130

Q: What do you call a baby potato?

A: A small fry.

• • • • • • • • • • • •

DAY 131

SCIENCE TEACHER: When is the boiling point reached?

STUDENT: When my mother sees my report card!

DAY 132

Q: What did the mother broom say to the baby broom?

A: "It's time to go to sweep!"

• • • • • • • • • • • •

DAY 133

Q: Did you hear the joke about Sean Connery's brother's newborn daughter?

A: It's a little niche.

• • • • • • • • • • • •

DAY 134

My friend's gambling habit is getting out of hand. The other day he tried to bet his newborn son in our game of poker, and I thought I might have to raise him.

DAY 135

Q: What's the fastest land mammal?

A: A toddler who's just been asked what's in their mouth.

• • • • • • • • • • • •

DAY 136

Q: Did you hear about the baby born in a high-tech hospital?

A: It arrived cordless.

DAD HACK: When changing a diaper, roll your baby's onesie over their arms to keep them from flailing around. It also makes them look like they're wearing a straitjacket, which is sweetly ironic since they're the one who's been driving you crazy.

DAY 137

Q: Why did the mother cross the road?

A: To get some peace and quiet!

• • • • • • • • • • • •

DAY 138

Q: What do you call a monkey's new baby?

A: A chimp off the old block.

• • • • • • • • • • • •

DAY 139

Q: What three words solve most dads' problems?

A: Ask your mother.

• • • • • • • • • • • •

DAY 140

Q: What do you call a group of baby garbage bins?

A: A litter.

DAY 141

I was worried that the hospital had accidentally switched our babies at birth. They're identical twins, so it's hard to be sure.

• • • • • • • • • • • • •

DAY 142

SON: Mom, what's a weekend?

MOM: I don't know, sweetheart, I haven't had one since you were born.

• • • • • • • • • • • • •

DAY 143

Q: How do you get an astronaut's baby to sleep?

A: You rocket.

DAY 144

Q: How many famous people were born on your birthday?

A: None—only babies.

DAY 145

Q: Why was the baby strawberry crying?

A: Its mom and dad were in a jam.

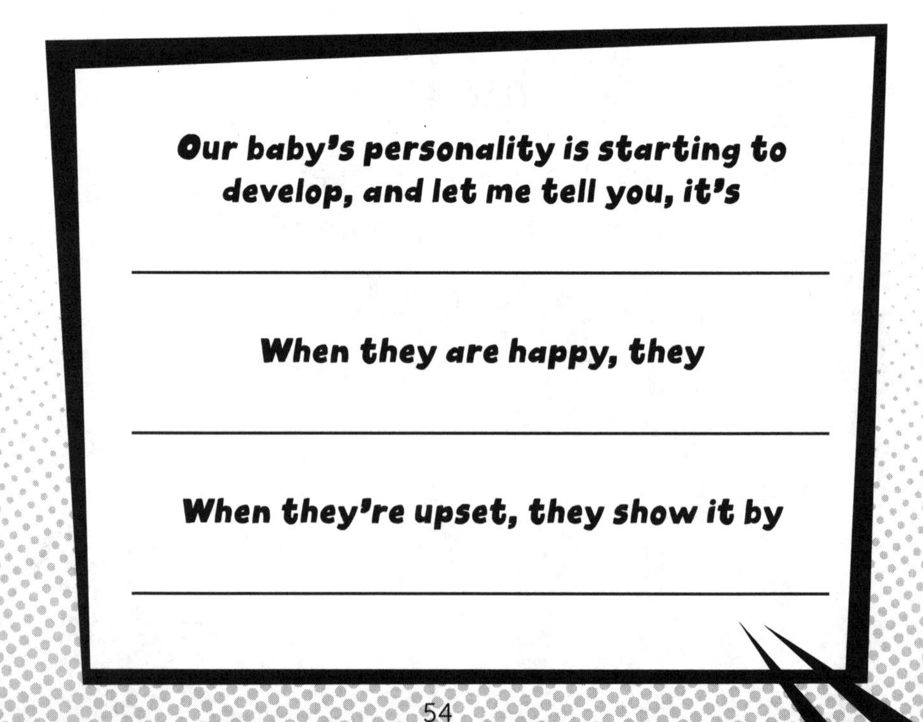

DAY 146

Q: How warm is a baby at birth?

A: Womb temperature.

• • • • • • • • • • • •

DAY 147

Q: When do parents change the most diapers?

A: In the wee-wee hours.

• • • • • • • • • • • •

DAY 148

Teddy came thundering down the stairs, much to his father's annoyance. "Teddy," he called, "how many more times have I got to tell you to come down the stairs quietly? Now, go back up and try it again." There was a silence, then Teddy reappeared in the front room without a sound. "That's better," said his father. "Now, will you always come downstairs like that?" "Suits me," said Teddy. "I slid down the bannister."

DAY 149

Q: What do thesauruses prefer for breakfast?

A: Synonym rolls.

• • • • • • • • • • • •

DAY 150

Q: Why did the fish blush?

A: It saw the ocean's bottom.

• • • • • • • • • • • •

DAY 151

Q: Why was the baby ink crying?

A: His mom was in the pen, and he didn't know how long her sentence was.

• • • • • • • • • • • •

DAY 152

The invisible man reconsidered a job offer. He just couldn't see himself doing it.

DAY 153

Q: What do you call a fake noodle?

A: An impasta.

• • • • • • • • • • • • • •

DAY 154

A steak pun is a rare medium done well.

DAD HACK: When your baby's first teeth appear, using a chilled teething ring often works best to soothe the pain and make them less cranky. You can also try rubbing a tiny amount of numbing gel around the budding tooth. If they are still fussy, you may consider using whiskey or rum . . . but only on yourself.

DAY 155

Q: Did you hear about the raisin that went out with the prune?

A: Couldn't find a date.

• • • • • • • • • • • •

DAY 156

An irate woman burst into the baker's shop and said, "I sent my son in for two pounds of cookies this morning, but when I weighed them, there was only one pound. I suggest that you check your scales." The baker looked at her calmly for a moment or two and then replied, "Ma'am, I suggest you weigh your son."

• • • • • • • • • • • •

DAY 157

Q: Who held the baby octopus ransom?

A: Squidnappers.

DAY 158

Q: What did the baby dolphin do when he didn't get his way?

A: He whaled.

• • • • • • • • • • • •

DAY 159

The other day I started a conversation with a dolphin. We just clicked.

• • • • • • • • • • • •

DAY 160

Q: What is a speech therapist's favorite brand of shoes?

A: Converse.

• • • • • • • • • • • •

DAY 161

The best nap time of the day is 6:30, hands down.

DAY 162

A banker kept pestering me with all kinds of offers. Finally, I told him to leave me a loan.

• • • • • • • • • • • •

DAY 163

Q: What is the benefit of being a test-tube baby?

A: Having a womb with a view.

• • • • • • • • • • • •

DAY 164

Amal and Juan are identical twins. Their mom carries only one baby photo in her wallet, because if you've seen Juan, you've seen Amal.

DAY 165

Q: What do snowmen do in their spare time?

A: They just chill.

• • • • • • • • • • • • •

DAY 166

I'm always a little nervous around calendars. Their days are numbered.

DAD HACK: While you're taking care of your baby, find the time to take care of each other, too. Hire a sitter for a few hours and go on a date. Bonus: While on your date, see how long before one of you talks about the baby. Treat yourself to dessert or a drink if you last 10 minutes.

DAY 167

Q: Dad, can you help me out?

A: Sure. Which way did you come in?

• • • • • • • • • • • •

DAY 168

A group of dads were remarking at how much Fred's baby daughter looked just like her mother. "They could be twins," one dad said. Fred replied, "Well, they were separated at birth!"

• • • • • • • • • • • •

DAY 169

Q: Did you hear about the kidnapping at school?

A: It's OK, he woke up.

DAY 170

Mr. and Mrs. Turner had a baby girl. They named her Paige since they just couldn't put her down.

• • • • • • • • • • • •

DAY 171

MRS. GOAT: Honey, we're going to have a baby!

MR. GOAT: You're kidding.

• • • • • • • • • • • •

DAY 172

Q: What does a skeleton say before dinner?

A: "Bone appétit."

• • • • • • • • • • • •

DAY 173

Q: Which friends are the best kind to eat with?

A: Your taste buds.

DAY 174

Q: How do you organize your baby's first birthday party in space?

A: You planet!

• • • • • • • • • • • •

DAY 175

SON: Dad, there is someone at the door to collect donations for a community swimming pool.

FATHER: OK, give him a glass of water.

• • • • • • • • • • • •

DAY 176

Q: Why don't crabs give to charity?

A: They're a real shellfish breed.

• • • • • • • • • • • •

DAY 177

Q: Have you ever tried to eat a clock?

A: It's very time-consuming.

DAY 178

Q: What does a computerized frog say?

A: "Reboot, reboot, reboot . . ."

• • • • • • • • • • • • •

DAY 179

Cannibals aren't very social.
They're fed up with people.

What I've learned most about myself as a father so far (aside from how much I value sleep) is

DAY 180

Q: What do you do when your boss tells you to have a good day?

A: Go home.

DAY 181

Q: What did the mother cow say to the baby cow?

A: "It's pasture bedtime."

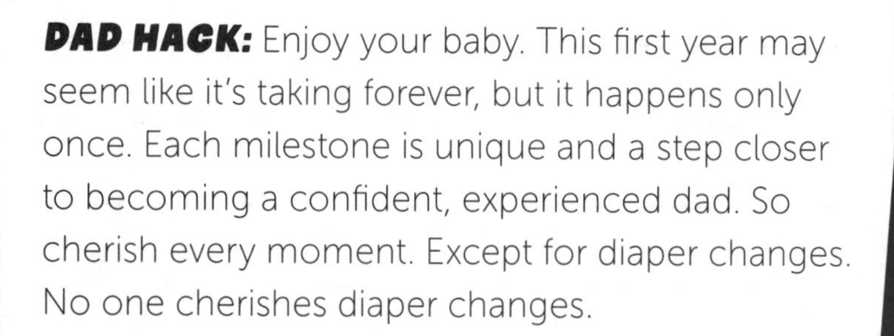

DAD HACK: Enjoy your baby. This first year may seem like it's taking forever, but it happens only once. Each milestone is unique and a step closer to becoming a confident, experienced dad. So cherish every moment. Except for diaper changes. No one cherishes diaper changes.

DAY 182

I spotted a lion today. Now it looks like a leopard.

• • • • • • • • • • • •

DAY 183

Q: Why is it impossible for new parents to change a light bulb?

A: Because they don't make diapers small enough.

• • • • • • • • • • • •

DAY 184

Q: What's the best way to watch a fly-fishing tournament?

A: Live stream.

DAY 185

As a student, Karl Marx was often teased by his classmates for his difficulty with capitalization.

• • • • • • • • • • • • •

DAY 186

A baby's laugh is one of the most beautiful things you will ever hear . . . unless it is 3:00 a.m., you're home alone, and you don't have a baby.

• • • • • • • • • • • • •

DAY 187

Q: How did the hipster burn his tongue?

A: He ate his food before it was cool.

• • • • • • • • • • • • •

DAY 188

A misspelling on a headstone is a grave mistake.

DAY 189

A good elevator joke works on so many levels.

DAY 190

Q: Why do melons have weddings?

A: Because they cantaloupe!

DAY 191

Q: Why can't a nose be 12 inches long?

A: Because then it would be a foot.

DAD HACK: If you need to mix things up, you'll find that the kitchen sink is the perfect height for a baby bathtub. Just don't throw the baby out with the dishwater.

DAY 192

I made a pencil with an eraser at both ends. It was pointless.

DAY 193

Q: What superpower do you get when you become a parent?

A: Supervision.

DAY 194

My friend keeps saying, "Cheer up, man. It could be worse—you could be stuck underground in a hole full of water." I know he means well.

DAY 195

Q: What did the windmill say when he met his favorite celebrity?

A: "Oh my gosh, I'm such a big fan!"

• • • • • • • • • • • • •

DAY 196

Q: What's the most solitary cheese in the world?

A: Provolone.

Our baby's food journey now includes solid food. Their favorite meal is

____

and their favorite snacks are

____

The food most likely to be thrown across the room is

____

DAY 197

I'd like to get a new boomerang, but I can't throw the old one away.

• • • • • • • • • • • •

DAY 198

Some kids like elevators; some like escalators. Depends on how they were raised.

• • • • • • • • • • • •

DAY 199

The wedding was so beautiful, even the cake was in tiers.

• • • • • • • • • • • •

DAY 200

Today I'm attaching a light to the ceiling, but I'll probably screw it up.

DAY 201

Q: What's the difference between ignorance and indifference?

A: I don't know, and I don't care.

DAY 202

Q: What do prisoners use to call each other?

A: Their cell phones.

DAY 203

Want to hear a joke about a piece of paper? Never mind . . . it's tearable.

DAD HACK: Most babies love to be gently bounced. Bouncy seats or even exercise balls work great for this. Trampolines, not so much.

DAY 204

Q: Why did the cops arrest the chicken?

A: They suspected fowl play.

• • • • • • • • • • • •

DAY 205

I hung a framed copy of the U.S. Constitution on my wall. It is a decoration of independence.

• • • • • • • • • • • •

DAY 206

Q: What do you call a dog that does magic tricks?

A: A labracadabrador.

DAY 207

Last week my partner and I built an igloo. Our friends came over and threw us a housewarming party. Now we're back to square one.

• • • • • • • • • • • •

DAY 208

Did you know the first french fries weren't cooked in France? They were cooked in Greece.

• • • • • • • • • • • •

DAY 209

Q: How did the pirate do in school?

A: He earned seven Cs on every report card.

DAY 210

Q: What is a pirate's favorite brand of baby food for their little one?

A: Gerrrberrr.

• • • • • • • • • • • •

DAY 211

Q: Why do pirates have trouble singing the alphabet?

A: They get lost at *C*.

• • • • • • • • • • • •

DAY 212

I told a coworker that I thought they drew their eyebrows in too high. They seemed surprised.

• • • • • • • • • • • •

DAY 213

Q: Where does light go when it's been bad?

A: To prism.

DAY 214

Sometimes when I have a moment to relax, I spend time looking at my ceiling. I'm not sure if it's the best ceiling in the world, but it's definitely up there.

• • • • • • • • • • • •

DAY 215

I think I might have bad posture, but it's just a hunch.

• • • • • • • • • • • •

DAY 216

Q: Why did the man fall down the well?

A: He didn't see that well.

DAD HACK: Ripped diaper tab? Don't throw the diaper away; just let this moment serve as a reminder that duct tape can solve most problems in life.

DAY 217

A friend of mine went to mime school, and I never heard from him again.

• • • • • • • • • • • • •

DAY 218

Q: What's the best part about living in Switzerland?

A: I'm not sure, but the flag is a big plus.

• • • • • • • • • • • • •

DAY 219

Q: What do you feed a newborn if you want her to be a race car driver?

A: Formula 1.

• • • • • • • • • • • • •

DAY 220

I decided to sell our vacuum cleaner. It was just gathering dust.

DAY 221

A man visited a film studio and was browsing the wardrobe archives. He asked a costume designer which were her favorite pieces. She replied, "Well, that shirt there was worn by Pacino. That jacket was put together for De Niro. And these boots were made for Walken."

• • • • • • • • • • • •

DAY 222

Not all babies are delivered by storks. Some of the larger ones require cranes.

• • • • • • • • • • • •

DAY 223

Q: Have you heard about the restaurant on the moon?

A: Great food, no atmosphere.

DAY 224

Q: What does a clock do when it's hungry?

A: It goes back four seconds.

• • • • • • • • • • • • • •

DAY 225

I can't stand elevators. They drive me up a wall.

• • • • • • • • • • • • • •

DAY 226

I ran out of clean pants this morning. I felt so depleated.

One thing I'll want to always remember about this time is

____

One thing I'll be happy to forget is

____

DAY 227

Q: What does garlic do when it gets hot?

A: Takes its cloves off.

• • • • • • • • • • • •

DAY 228

After 65 years of marriage, my grandpa still calls my grandma "honey," "sweetie," "baby," and "sugar." I asked him for the secret to keeping love alive so long. He said, "I forgot her name 10 years ago, and I'm too afraid to ask."

• • • • • • • • • • • •

DAY 229

Mountains aren't just funny. They're hill areas.

DAY 230

Q: What do you call a baby that turns into a frog?

A: A toadler.

DAY 231

Dogs don't make great dancers. They have two left feet.

DAY 232

Never cheat at limbo. It's one of the lowest things you could do.

DAD HACK: Be sure to baby-proof all doors, cabinets, and drawers in the house. It's also fun to see how many adults have trouble navigating these devices.

DAY 233

Q: Why are skeletons so calm?

A: Nothing gets under their skin.

• • • • • • • • • • • • •

DAY 234

A couple has a baby. For four years he makes no sound and does not speak. Then one day the mother gives him soup, and he says, "This soup is cold." The parents are amazed and ask, "If you can talk, why have you not spoken up before?" The child replies, "Up to now everything has been great!"

• • • • • • • • • • • • •

DAY 235

I once skipped school to go bungee jumping with friends. We all got suspended.

DAY 236

Q: What do you call a wandering caveman?

A: A meanderthal.

• • • • • • • • • • • • •

DAY 237

I want to organize a hide-and-seek league, but good players are hard to find.

• • • • • • • • • • • • •

DAY 238

Q: Why did the chicken cross the playground?

A: To get to the other slide.

• • • • • • • • • • • • •

DAY 239

I thought culinary school was going to be difficult, but the final exam was a piece of cake.

DAY 240

A worried new mother consults her friend. "Since I had the baby, I can't sleep at night. When I'm in the next room, I have this dreadful fear that I won't hear the baby if he falls out of the crib at night. What should I do?" "Easy," her friend says. "Just take the carpet off the floor."

• • • • • • • • • • • •

DAY 241

Q: Did you hear about my neighbor?

A: 50 years old, delivers babies for a living, just bought a new car. Classic midwife crisis.

• • • • • • • • • • • •

DAY 242

Q: How do you get a good price on a sled?

A: You have toboggan.

DAY 243

Q: What do you call a fly without wings?

A: A walk.

DAY 244

I was going to tell a time-traveling joke, but you didn't like it.

DAY 245

Nine months isn't that long, although it can feel like a maternity.

DAD HACK: Make a little basket of diaper-changing supplies that you can carry around the home with you. It will come in handy when you hear an explosive poo from across the room and you realize that moving your baby might be a hazard worth avoiding.

DAY 246

Q: Why do dogs float in water?

A: Because they are good buoys.

• • • • • • • • • • • •

DAY 247

Singing in the shower is fun until you get soap in your mouth. Then it's a soap opera.

• • • • • • • • • • • •

DAY 248

Q: What do you call 52 slices of bread?

A: A deck of carbs.

• • • • • • • • • • • •

DAY 249

Q: Why do chicken coops have only two doors?

A: Because if they had four, they'd be chicken sedans.

DAY 250

I went to a Kleptomaniacs Anonymous meeting, but all the seats were taken.

• • • • • • • • • • • •

DAY 251

Q: How does Darth Vader like his toast?

A: On the dark side.

• • • • • • • • • • • •

DAY 252

Q: How should you greet your sibling's baby girl?

A: "Niece to meet you."

• • • • • • • • • • • •

DAY 253

Today, my son asked, "Can I have a bookmark?" and I burst into tears. He's 11 years old, and he still doesn't know my name is Brian.

DAY 254

Q: What has four legs and goes, "Booo"?

A: A cow with a cold.

DAY 255

Q: Why are snails bad at racing?

A: They can be sluggish.

DAY 256

I kept wondering why the Frisbee was getting larger. Then it hit me.

• • • • • • • • • • • • • •

DAY 257

I encouraged my son to tie his own shoelaces today. He did an OK job. In fact, it was knot bad.

• • • • • • • • • • • • • •

DAY 258

Q: Is this pool safe for diving?

A: It deep ends.

DAD HACK: If you are bottle-feeding, instead of going to the kitchen in the middle of the night, keep a little cooler next to your bed. And when your baby outgrows this need, you now have easy access to a cold one.

DAY 259

People who refuse to learn math rarely amount to anything.

• • • • • • • • • • • •

DAY 260

A man goes to a funeral and asks the widow, "Mind if I say a word?" "Please do," she says. The man clears his throat and says, "Earth." The widow replies, "Thank you. That means the world to me."

• • • • • • • • • • • •

DAY 261

Q: What do you call an anxious dinosaur?

A: A Nervous rex.

• • • • • • • • • • • •

DAY 262

I tried to make Hawaiian pizza, but I burned it. I should have known to use aloha setting.

DAY 263

My friends all claim I'm the cheapest person they've ever met. I'm not buying it.

• • • • • • • • • • • •

DAY 264

My new neighbors haven't put house numbers on their home yet. They really should address that.

• • • • • • • • • • • •

DAY 265

My friend said he didn't understand what cloning is. I said that makes two of us.

DAD HACK: Buy a label maker and label every generic bin in the house that contains baby supplies. It's also fun to make labels like "Spare Hand Grenades" or "Lightsaber Training Manuals" just to keep everyone on their toes.

DAY 266

Q: Why do seagulls fly over the sea?

A: If they flew over the bay, they'd be called bagels.

• • • • • • • • • • • •

DAY 267

Someone has been kidnapping the dogs in our neighborhood. The police say they have several leads.

• • • • • • • • • • • •

DAY 268

I finished my first week of excavation training. So far, I'm really digging it.

• • • • • • • • • • • •

DAY 269

Ghosts are such bad liars. You can see right through them.

DAY 270

Q: Did you hear about the couple who spent $1,000 on their front door?

A: Always making a grand entrance.

• • • • • • • • • • • •

DAY 271

"Mom, are bugs good to eat?" asked the boy. "Let's not talk about such things at the dinner table, son," his mother replied. After dinner, the mother asked, "Now, baby, what did you want to ask me?" "Oh, nothing," the boy said. "There was a bug in your soup, but now it's gone."

• • • • • • • • • • • •

DAY 272

I spent a lot of time, money,
and effort kid-proofing the house . . .
but the kids still get in.

DAY 273

My wife said I was immature, so I told her to get out of my fort.

• • • • • • • • • • • • •

DAY 274

I was having difficulty fastening my seat belt, and then it just clicked.

• • • • • • • • • • • • •

DAY 275

When I was a kid, my mom told me I could be anyone I wanted. Turns out identity theft is a crime.

• • • • • • • • • • • • •

DAY 276

Q: Why was Pavlov's hair so soft?

A: He conditioned it.

DAY 277

I was just reminiscing about the beautiful herb garden I had growing up. Good thymes.

• • • • • • • • • • • • •

DAY 278

Q: Do you know the last thing my grandfather said to me before he kicked the bucket?

A: "Grandson, watch how far I can kick this bucket."

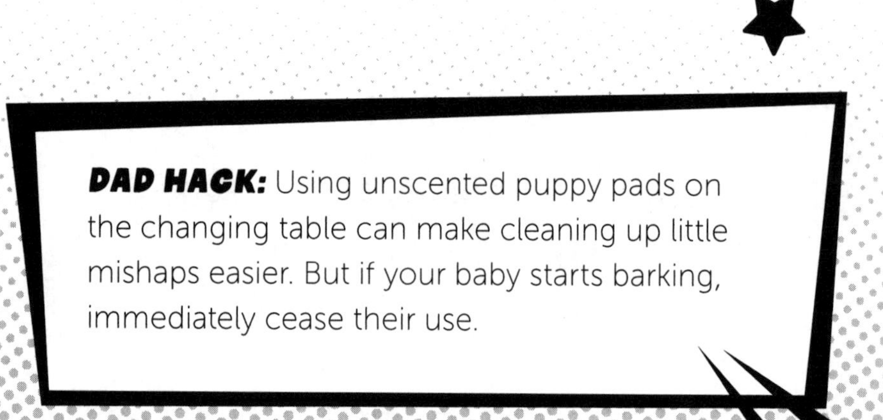

DAD HACK: Using unscented puppy pads on the changing table can make cleaning up little mishaps easier. But if your baby starts barking, immediately cease their use.

DAY 279

A kid asks his dad, "What's a man?" The dad says, "A man is someone who is responsible and cares for his family." The kid says, "I hope one day I can be a man just like Mom!"

• • • • • • • • • • • • •

DAY 280

Q: Why did the cowboy ride the horse?

A: Carrying the horse was out of the question.

• • • • • • • • • • • • •

DAY 281

Sore throats are a pain in the neck.

• • • • • • • • • • • • •

DAY 282

They say that 4/3 of people are bad at fractions.

DAY 283

Q: What did the janitor say when he popped out of the closet?

A: "Supplies!"

• • • • • • • • • • • •

DAY 284

Q: What did one math textbook say to the other?

A: "Dude, we've got a lot of problems."

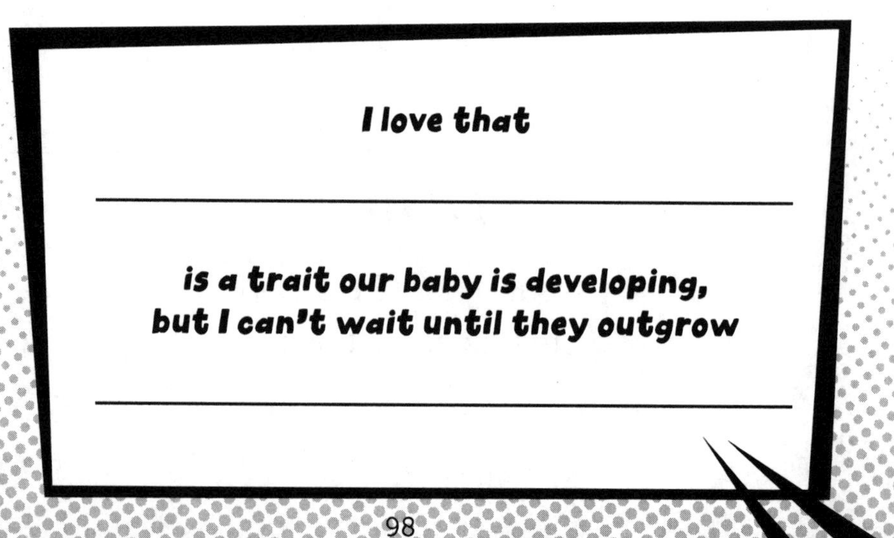

DAY 285

I installed a bar on my roof. Now I enjoy telling my guests that their drinks are on the house.

• • • • • • • • • • • •

DAY 286

My partner caught me kicking ice cubes that had fallen on the kitchen floor underneath the refrigerator. At first, she was annoyed. Now it's water under the fridge.

• • • • • • • • • • • •

DAY 287

My son was determined to climb the stairs, so I wrote him a step-by-step guide.

• • • • • • • • • • • •

DAY 288

Q: Can February march?

A: No, but April may.

DAY 289

Q: What do you get when you cross a sorcerer with a billionaire?

A: A very witch person.

• • • • • • • • • • • •

DAY 290

I just found out I'm color-blind. The diagnosis came out of the green.

• • • • • • • • • • • •

DAY 291

I wrote a joke about German sausages, but it was the wurst.

• • • • • • • • • • • •

DAY 292

Q: Did you hear about the sandwich that couldn't stop telling jokes?

A: It was on a roll.

DAY 293

I'm so good at sleeping that I do it with my eyes closed.

• • • • • • • • • • • •

DAY 294

As I handed my aunt her 50th birthday card, she became emotional and said, "You know, one card would have been enough."

DAD HACK: Something as simple as playing peekaboo—and showing your baby that you always come back after you disappear—can help your developing child cope with separation anxiety. Only time will tell if it helps you cope with yours, too.

DAY 295

Q: Did you hear about the award given to the inventor of the knock-knock joke?

A: Yeah, the No Bell Prize.

• • • • • • • • • • • • •

DAY 296

If towels could tell jokes, they'd have a very dry sense of humor.

• • • • • • • • • • • • •

DAY 297

Q: Where can you find the most superheroes in one place?

A: Cape Town.

• • • • • • • • • • • • •

DAY 298

I slept like a log last night. Woke up in the fireplace!

DAY 299

Q: Why did the stadium get so hot after the game?

A: All of the fans left.

• • • • • • • • • • • • •

DAY 300

I used to run a dating service for chickens, but I was struggling to make hens meet.

• • • • • • • • • • • • •

DAY 301

A man heard about a gold rush in California. He quit his job, packed up his belongings, and headed out west. But after a year of unsuccessful mining, he returned home penniless. Just didn't pan out.

DAY 302

Q: How do you make a waterbed bouncier?

A: Fill it with spring water.

• • • • • • • • • • • •

DAY 303

They say the desserts in Italy are the best in the world. I've never been, so I cannoli imagine.

• • • • • • • • • • • •

DAY 304

Not to brag, but I made seven figures last year. Turns out I was the worst employee at the toy factory.

• • • • • • • • • • • •

DAY 305

Q: What rhymes with orange?

A: No, it doesn't.

DAY 306

Q: What did the two pieces of bread say on their wedding day?

A: "It was loaf at first sight."

• • • • • • • • • • • •

DAY 307

Someone complimented my parking today. They left a sweet note on the windshield that said, "Parking fine."

DAD HACK: When buying clothes for your baby, preserve your sanity by choosing zippers over buttons. You'll be less likely to snap.

DAY 308

Some people can't tell the difference between entomology and etymology. They bug me in ways I can't put into words.

• • • • • • • • • • • •

DAY 309

Q: What do you call a Frenchman wearing sandals?

A: Philippe Flop.

• • • • • • • • • • • •

DAY 310

Geology rocks, but geography is where it's at.

• • • • • • • • • • • •

DAY 311

I don't always give away my used batteries, but when I do, they're free of charge.

DAY 312

I hate it when people say age is just a number. Age is clearly a word.

DAY 313

Q: What is a trombone's range?

A: About 20 yards, if you've got a good arm.

DAY 314

If you rearrange the letters of POSTMEN, they become very angry.

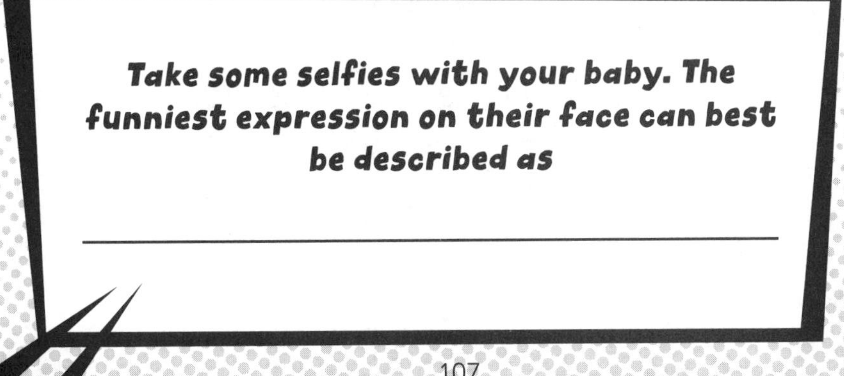

DAY 315

Q: Did you hear about those new corduroy pillows?

A: They're making headlines.

• • • • • • • • • • • •

DAY 316

I want to warn the person who stole my glasses, I have many contacts.

• • • • • • • • • • • •

DAY 317

Q: Why did the composer stay in bed?

A: To finish writing their sheet music.

• • • • • • • • • • • •

DAY 318

Q: Did you hear the conspiracy theory about two single beds?

A: It was debunked.

DAY 319

To the person who stole my place in line: I'm after you now.

• • • • • • • • • • • •

DAY 320

Q: What do you call a fashion designer who refuses to listen to you?

A: Clothes-minded.

DAD HACK: Find a dad support group that has regular meetings. Some moms are suspicious that these groups are just excuses for men to get together and party, but plenty of legitimate organizations exist for the purpose of dads supporting one another. And if some members choose to bring snacks and a poker table, so be it.

DAY 321

I can't stress enough the importance of developing a strong vocabulary. If I had known the difference between the words *antidote* and *anecdote*, one of my best friends would still be alive.

• • • • • • • • • • • •

DAY 322

Q: How do you deal with a fear of speed bumps?

A: You slowly get over it.

• • • • • • • • • • • •

DAY 323

I only know 25 letters of the alphabet. I don't know *Y*.

DAY 324

Q: Did you hear about the circus fire?

A: It was in tents!

• • • • • • • • • • • •

DAY 325

A travel agent told me they could get me a free trip to Egypt if I could get five other people to also sign up. It sounded like a pyramid scheme.

• • • • • • • • • • • •

DAY 326

Q: What state is known for its small drinks?

A: Minnesota.

• • • • • • • • • • • •

DAY 327

I just bought my daughter her first watch. She said it was about time.

DAY 328

Q: What's Forrest Gump's password?

A: 1forrest1

. . . .

DAY 329

A group of chess enthusiasts checked in to a hotel and were standing in the lobby discussing their recent tournament victories. After about an hour, the manager came out of the office and asked them to disperse. "But why?" they asked. "Because," he said, "I can't stand chess nuts boasting in an open foyer."

. . . .

DAY 330

Q: How did the tree stay in shape?

A: It did planks.

DAY 331

I heard that diarrhea can be hereditary if it runs in your jeans.

• • • • • • • • • • • • • •

DAY 332

I decided to take up fencing. The neighbors say they'll call the authorities unless I put it back.

DAD HACK: Use nose hair scissors to trim your baby's nails. You may also use a nail file. Never chew on your baby's nails to remove them. After all, you don't really know where they've been.

DAY 333

Q: What do you call a beehive without an exit?

A: Unbelievable.

• • • • • • • • • • • •

DAY 334

Never trust atoms. They make up everything.

• • • • • • • • • • • •

DAY 335

I was recently hired to run the Old MacDonald Farm. I'm the C-I-E-I-O.

• • • • • • • • • • • •

DAY 336

As a lumberjack, I'm certain that I've cut down exactly 2,417 trees, because every time I cut one, I keep a log.

DAY 337

Time flies like an arrow. Fruit
flies like a banana.

• • • • • • • • • • • •

DAY 338

Q: Did you hear about the bored banker?

A: They lost interest in everything.

• • • • • • • • • • • •

DAY 339

Q: Can a kangaroo jump
higher than a house?

A: Of course! Houses can't jump.

• • • • • • • • • • • •

DAY 340

I never buy preshredded cheese
because shredding it yourself is grate.

DAY 341

I was playing chess with a friend, and she said, "Let's make this interesting." So we stopped playing.

• • • • • • • • • • • •

DAY 342

Q: What do scholars eat when they're hungry?

A: Academia nuts.

• • • • • • • • • • • •

DAY 343

I vacationed at a haunted bed-and-breakfast in France. The place gave me the crepes.

• • • • • • • • • • • •

DAY 344

My recliner and I go way back.

Dear ______________________________,

This first year I did my best
to be a good dad to you by

____

____

____

____

____

____

I hope you forgive me for that one time I

____

____

____

____

____

____

____

DAY 345

At first, my dad didn't like the swivel chair I bought him. But after sitting in it for a while, he came around.

• • • • • • • • • • • •

DAY 346

To the person who invented zero: Thanks for nothing.

• • • • • • • • • • • •

DAY 347

Q: What do you call an ant shunned by its community?

A: Socially dissed ant.

• • • • • • • • • • • •

DAY 348

Autocorrect causes me to say things I didn't Nintendo.

DAY 349

Q: What happens when a Finnish passenger jumps from a cruise ship?

A: Helsinki.

• • • • • • • • • • • •

DAY 350

A dad submitted 10 different puns to a joke contest sponsored by a local newspaper. He hoped that at least one would make the final round. Unfortunately, no pun in 10 did.

• • • • • • • • • • • •

DAY 351

Q: How many apples grow on a tree?

A: All of them.

DAY 352

When I was young, I wanted to make the perfect bar of soap, but that dream slipped away.

• • • • • • • • • • • •

DAY 353

My friend broke my pen, but he promised me he would make it write.

• • • • • • • • • • • •

DAY 354

I'm not saying ancient history lecturers are boring; they just tend to Babylon.

• • • • • • • • • • • •

DAY 355

Q: What's blue and doesn't weigh very much?

A: Light blue.

DAY 356

Q: Which bear is the most condescending?

A: A pan, duh.

DAY 357

I asked my son, "What's two minus two?" He said nothing.

DAY 358

Milk is the fastest liquid in the world. It's pasteurized before you can see it.

DAD HACK: Take time to remind yourself that crying is a normal part of your baby's first year. Eventually, you will grow out of it.

DAY 359

If two vegetarians get into an argument, is it still called beef?

• • • • • • • • • • • •

DAY 360

Q: Did you hear about the dad hospitalized after a game of peekaboo?

A: They put him in the ICU.

• • • • • • • • • • • •

DAY 361

If the early bird gets the worm, I'll sleep until there's pancakes.

• • • • • • • • • • • •

DAY 362

At my age, I'm no longer a snack; I'm a Happy Meal. I come with toys and kids.

DAY 363

DAUGHTER: I'll call you later.

DAD: Don't call me Later; call me Dad!

• • • • • • • • • • • •

DAY 364

I love telling dad jokes.
Sometimes he even laughs.

• • • • • • • • • • • •

DAY 365

Q: Did you hear about the cat that ate a ball of yarn?

A: She had mittens.

ABOUT THE AUTHOR

SLADE WENTWORTH is a writer and creative entrepreneur who'd rather be cooking with his kids. You can follow his dad humor and family recipes on Instagram and TikTok **@THEDADBRIEFS**.

Hi there,

We hope you enjoyed *New Dad, Same Bad Jokes*. If you have any questions or concerns about your book, or have received a damaged copy, please contact **customerservice@penguinrandomhouse.com**. We're here and happy to help.

Also, please consider writing a review on your favorite retailer's website to let others know what you thought of the book!

Sincerely,
The Zeitgeist Team